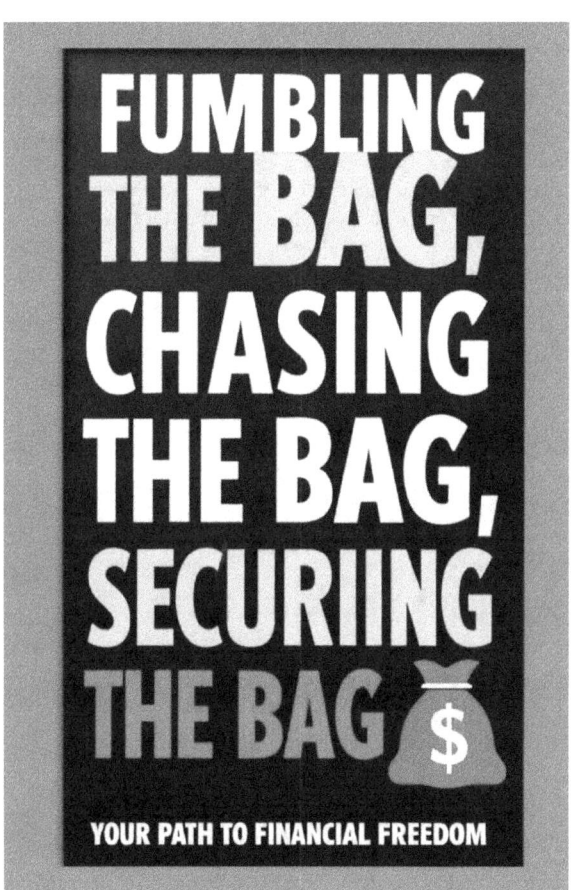

Copyright © 2024 by Brian Ernest Hayward and Published by Brian Hayward for Hayward House Publishing Published by Hayward House and Big Book Box A Member of the Brian Hayward Group All rights reserved. No part of this publication may be reproduced, stored in a retrieval system, or transmitted, in any form or by any means, electronic, mechanical, photocopying, recording, or otherwise, without the prior written permission of the publisher. For information and inquiries , address Hayward House publishing and Hayward Press, Savannah, Ga 31405, Library of Congress Cataloging-in-Publication Data. Hayward, Brian. TITLE=In Jesus Mighty Name Series, Journal WRITING for success in your life / Brian Hayward. p. cm.

PAPERBACK EDITION

ISBN: 9798333626493
Imprint:
Independently published

Self-control. 2. Self-management (Psychology) 3. Success. 4. Success in business. 31405, or visit us at https://www.amazon.com/Brian-Ernest-Hayward/e/B06XT464NM

PRAYER FOR MYSELF AND MY READERS

I was taught by my teacher, Pastor Bill Winston, this prayer. This prayer has served me well, and in due time it will serve you well. Father I come before you in Jesus name, thank you for the anointing that's on me and these lips of clay. I know that because of your blessing, I speak this word today with excellency, accuracy, and boldness. I thank you for thinking through my mind and speaking through my lips and this word will come forth unhindered, and unchecked by any outside force. Now I give you the praise for it and I fully expect signs, wonders, and miracles to confirm your word preached in Jesus name,

AUTHOR BIOGRAPHY

Brian Ernest Hayward is a passionate Author and Inspirational Speaker, internationally known for his unwavering dedication to creating positive change through the power of words. From religious and success books, to adult coloring books and artist BUSINESS, HOW-TO BOOKS, his writings touch on over 400 different subjects. Today, all of Brian's publications are sold worldwide across multiple formats (Paperback, Kindle, and Large Print) and are translated into 21 different languages. He has also participated in over 100 speaking engagements spanning over 38 states.

Table Of Contents

Introduction — 6

Chapter 1: "Fumbling the Bag: The Anatomy of Financial Failures — 16

Chapter 2: Reevaluating Your Financial Habits — 23

Chapter 3: CHASING THE BAG: Financial Self-Assessment Tools — 33

Chapter 4: SECURING THE BAG: Emergency Funds and Savings Strategies — 41

Chapter 5: CHASING THE BAG: Exploring Alternative Revenue Streams — 50

Chapter 6: Basic Principles of Financial Planning — 58

Chapter 7: Understanding Credit and Loans — 66

Chapter 8: SECURING THE BAG: Effective Money Management Systems ... 74

Chapter 9: SECURING THE BAG: Planning for the Unexpected ... 82

Chapter 10: SECURING THE BAG: Achieving Financial Independence ... 90

Conclusion ... 98

Bibliography ... 114

Introduction

Welcome to "Fumbling the Bag, Chasing the Bag, Securing the Bag: From Setbacks to Comebacks: Your Path to Financial Freedom." If you've ever felt like your financial life is a never-ending sitcom of bloopers, this book is your guide to turning those laughable missteps into applause-worthy successes.

Authoring this book was a labor of love, sweat, and a few tears, taking a full three months to compile all the wisdom, humor, and practical advice you'll find within these pages. Each month was dedicated to a different aspect of creating this masterpiece manual, ensuring every chapter was packed with valuable insights and actionable steps.

In the first month, we dove headfirst into research. Countless hours were spent poring over financial studies, interviewing experts, and analyzing real-life case studies of economic mismanagement. The goal was to understand the root causes of financial setbacks and the psychological impacts of financial stress. This foundational knowledge is critical for anyone looking to improve their financial situation, as it provides the context needed to make informed decisions and avoid common pitfalls.

The second month was dedicated to developing practical strategies. We wanted this book to be more than just a collection of financial theories; it needed to be a practical guide that  anyone could follow. This involved creating detailed plans for budgeting, saving, investing, and managing debt. We also explored various income generation strategies, from side hustles to passive income ideas. The result is a comprehensive toolkit that you can use to build a strong financial foundation and achieve your goals.

The third and final month was all about refinement and presentation. We wanted this book to be not only informative but also engaging and entertaining. This meant adding a touch of humor to make the content more relatable and enjoyable to read. We also worked on the structure, ensuring that each chapter flows smoothly into the next and that the information is presented in a clear, easy-to-understand manner. The result is a book that is both educational and entertaining, providing you with the knowledge and motivation you need to take control of your financial future.

Why is this book needed? Financial literacy is more important than ever in today's fast-paced, consumer-driven world. Many people find themselves fumbling the bag—making poor financial decisions that lead to stress and hardship. This book addresses people's common mistakes and provides practical solutions to help you chase and secure the bag. Following the principles outlined in this manual can turn setbacks into comebacks and achieve financial freedom.

What sets this book apart is its focus on real-world application. The strategies and techniques we discuss are not just theoretical; they are practical steps you can implement daily. Whether you're dealing with debt, trying to save for a big purchase, or looking to invest for the future, this book provides actionable advice you can use immediately. The goal is to empower you to take control of your finances and achieve your goals.

When is this book relevant? The principles of fiscal management are timeless. Whether you're just starting out in your career, planning for retirement, or somewhere in between, the strategies in this book can help you navigate the financial challenges you face. The advice is designed to be flexible and adaptable, so you can apply it to your unique situation and needs.

Where can you apply the concepts in this book? The strategies and techniques we discuss are applicable in a wide range of situations. Whether you are managing your finances, running a small business, or planning, budgeting, saving, investing, and managing debt are universally relevant. This book provides a roadmap that you can follow to achieve financial success in any context.

How can you apply the concepts in this book? Each chapter is packed with practical tips and actionable steps that you can implement right away. From creating a budget and building an emergency fund to exploring alternative revenue streams and investing wisely,  this book provides a step-by-step guide to achieving your financial goals. Following this book's advice lets you take control of your finances and create a more secure and prosperous future.

"Fumbling the Bag, Chasing the Bag, Securing the Bag" is about turning financial missteps into success stories. It recognizes that everyone makes mistakes, but how you respond to those mistakes determines your financial future. This book provides the tools and strategies to bounce back from and build a solid foundation. Whether you are struggling with debt, trying to save for a big purchase, or looking to invest in the future, this book provides the guidance and support you need to achieve your goals.

The principles outlined in this book are crucial in day-to-day business. Fiscal management is an essential aspect of running a successful business, and the strategies we discuss can help you make informed decisions, manage cash flow, and plan. Whether you are a small business owner or an entrepreneur, the advice in this book can help you navigate the financial challenges you face and achieve your business goals.

This book is not just about avoiding financial mistakes; it is about creating a roadmap for success. It is about understanding the importance of financial literacy and taking proactive steps to improve your financial situation. Following the principles outlined in this book can create a more secure and prosperous future for yourself and your loved ones.

Readers will fall in love with this book because of its friendly, humorous tone and practical advice. It is like conversing with a knowledgeable friend  who genuinely wants to help you succeed. The engaging writing style makes complex financial concepts easy to understand and enjoyable to read. This book is not just a manual; it is a companion on your journey to financial freedom.

In conclusion, "Fumbling the Bag, Chasing the Bag, Securing the Bag: From Setbacks to Comebacks: Your Path to Financial Freedom" is a comprehensive guide to improving your financial situation. It provides practical strategies, actionable steps, and a touch of humor to make the journey enjoyable.

Whether you're dealing with debt, trying to save for a big purchase, or looking to invest for the future, this book provides the guidance and support you need to achieve your goals. Following the principles outlined in this book can turn setbacks into comebacks and achieve financial freedom.

Chapter 1: "Fumbling the Bag: The Anatomy of Financial Failures

Financial failures are like a bad haircut; they happen to the best of us and often when we least expect them. Identifying the root causes of financial setbacks is the first step toward recovery.  A few culprits are poor budgeting, unexpected expenses, and bad investments. Often, people fumble the bag due to a lack of financial literacy. It's not that they don't want to be responsible; it's just that they don't know how. This chapter aims to dissect these failures with a surgeon's precision, highlighting common pitfalls and how to avoid them.

The psychological impacts of financial stress are immense. Money worries can keep you up at night, strain your relationships, and even affect your physical health. Understanding the mental toll is crucial because financial decisions are rarely made in a vacuum. When stressed, you're more likely to make impulsive decisions, exacerbating the problem. Recognizing this psychological component can help you stay calm and make more rational choices in the face of financial difficulties.

One of the most insightful ways to learn is through case studies of financial mismanagement. Take John, for example. He invested heavily in a friend's startup without doing proper research. When the company tanked, he  lost his savings and had to move back in with his parents. Or consider Sarah, who ignored her mounting credit card debt until the interest alone was overwhelming. These stories, while unfortunate, serve as powerful lessons in what not to do. They illustrate the importance of due diligence and the dangers of ignoring financial red flags.

Another essential critical is understanding how small, insignificant decisions can snowball into major financial disasters. It's like eating one cookie daily; it doesn't seem like much until you realize you've gained ten pounds. Small purchases, when unchecked, can lead to significant debt. This chapter will teach you to recognize and curb these habits before they spiral out of control.

Recognizing the difference between wants and needs is essential. It's a simple concept but one that many struggle with. Do you need that new iPhone, or do you want it? This chapter will guide you through exercises to help differentiate between the two, leading to better spending habits. By focusing on needs, you can save more and reduce unnecessary expenditures.

The role of peer pressure in financial decisions cannot be overstated. We live in a world where social media flaunts the latest trends and luxury lifestyles, making it easy to fall into the trap of keeping up with the Joneses. Understanding this influence can help you make more grounded financial decisions. If it means staying within your budget, say no to that weekend trip if resisting peer pressure is vital in securing your financial future.

Another critical factor is the lack of financial education in our school systems. Most people graduate without knowing how to balance a checkbook or file taxes. This knowledge gap leaves many ill-prepared for real-world financial responsibilities. This chapter will discuss ways to avoid principles and economics. With proper knowledge, you can avoid common pitfalls and make informed decisions.

Impulse buying is another common cause of financial failure. The thrill of a new purchase can be addictive, but it often leads to buyer's remorse and depleted bank accounts. Learning to manage impulses through techniques like the 24-hour rule—waiting a day before making a purchase—can save you a lot of money eventually. This chapter will provide practical tips to help you curb impulsive spending and stick to your budget.

Understanding the importance of an emergency fund cannot be overstated. Life is unpredictable, and having a financial cushion can mean the difference between a minor setback and a major catastrophe. This chapter will guide you through setting up an email to maintain an emergency fund and think of it as a financial safety net that catches you when life throws you a curveball.

Bad investments are another common cause of financial setbacks. Whether it's a shady stock tip or an overhyped cryptocurrency, investing without proper research is like playing Russian roulette with your money. This chapter will teach you how to evaluate investment opportunities critically. By understanding the basics of risk and reward, you can make smarter investment choices contributing to long-term financial stability.

Credit card debt is a financial pitfall that many fall into. It's easy to swipe now and worry about paying later, but this mentality can lead to insurmountable debt. This chapter will explore the dangers of credit card misuse and provide strategies for managing and reducing debt. You can avoid the credit card trap by understanding how interest works and the importance of timely payments.

The role of financial goals in preventing setbacks is crucial. Without clear goals, losing track of your financial path is easy. This chapter will help you set realistic, achievable financial goals. Whether it's saving for a house, a car, or retirement, having a clear target can guide your financial decisions and keep you motivated.

Budgeting is the cornerstone of financial success, yet many people neglect it. This chapter will break down the budgeting process into simple, manageable steps. You can create a budget that works for you by tracking your income and expenses. Budgeting doesn't have to be restrictive; it's about making your money work for you and achieving your financial goals.

Understanding financial products is essential for avoiding setbacks. Knowing what you're getting into can save you a lot of trouble, from loans to insurance. This chapter will demystify everyday financial products and explain how they can be used effectively. With the proper knowledge, you can make informed decisions and avoid products that don't serve your best interests.

Finally, this chapter will emphasize the importance of seeking professional advice. Sometimes, the best way to avoid a financial setback is to consult with a financial advisor. They can provide personalized guidance to help you navigate complex financial situations. Don't be afraid to ask for help; it could be your best investment in your financial future.

Chapter 2: Reevaluating Your Financial Habits

Reevaluating your financial habits is like spring cleaning for your finances; it might seem daunting, but it's gratifying. The first step is analyzing your spending patterns. Take a good, hard look at where your money is going each month. You might be surprised at how much you're spending on non-essentials. This  chapter will guide you through creating a spending diary to track every penny. By doing this, you'll identify patterns and areas where you can cut back.

Breaking bad financial habits is no small feat, but it's entirely possible with effort and dedication. Start by identifying the habits that are draining your wallet. It's that daily latte or those late-night online shopping sprees. Once you've pinpointed these habits, you can work on breaking them. This chapter will provide practical tips and strategies to help you replace unpleasant habits with good ones. It's all about making small, manageable changes that add up over time.

Setting The next step is to develop sensitive financial behaviors. Think of it as rewiring your brain to make better financial decisions. This chapter will introduce techniques like setting up automatic savings transfers and using apps to monitor spending. By incorporating these behaviors into your daily routine, you create a sturdy foundation for financial success. It's about making sound financial habits second nature.

One effective way to change your financial habits is through goal setting. Set clear, achievable goals for your finances. Whether paying off a credit card, saving for a vacation, or building an emergency fund, having specific goals can keep you motivated. This chapter will guide you through the process of achieving financial goals. Remember, it's not about perfection; it's about progress.

Accountability is crucial in reevaluating your financial habits. Find someone you trust, whether a friend or family financial advisor and share your goals with them. Having someone to check in with can help keep you on track. This chapter will explore ways to stay on track, from active, holy check-ins to financial support groups. Accountability partners can provide encouragement and keep you focused on your financial journey.

The role of technology in managing finances has grown tremendously. There are countless apps and tools. Countless tracks your spending, create a budget, and even invest. This chapter will  review some of the best financial apps available and show you how to use them effectively. By leveraging technology, you can streamline your fiscal management and make it easier to stay on top of your money.

Understanding the psychology behind spending is essential. Many of us spend money to fulfill emotional needs rather than practical ones. This chapter will delve into the psychological triggers that lead to overspending. By understanding these triggers, you can develop strategies to manage them. Whether it's stress, boredom, or the desire to impress others, recognizing your spending triggers is the first step to overcoming them.

Impulse control is a significant factor in financial health. We live in a world of instant gratification, but economic success often requires delayed gratification. This chapter will provide techniques to help you control impulsive spending. From waiting 24 hours before making a purchase to creating a list of financial priorities, these strategies can help you stay disciplined and focused on your long-term goals.

The importance of living below your means cannot be overstated. It's a simple concept but a powerful one. Spend less than you earn and save the rest. This chapter will explore reducing your living expenses without sacrificing your quality of life. From cooking at home to finding free entertainment, there are countless ways to enjoy life without breaking the bank.

Building a frugal mindset is another crucial aspect of reevaluating your financial habits. Frugality doesn't mean being cheap; it means being smart with your money. This chapter will teach you how to adopt a frugal mindset and maximize what you have. By focusing on value rather than cost, you can make better financial decisions that benefit you overall.

Creating a financial plan is essential for long-term success. This chapter will guide you through the process of developing a comprehensive financial plan. From setting goals to tracking progress, a financial plan provides a roadmap for your financial journey. By having a clear plan, you can stay focused and motivated, knowing that every step you take brings you closer to your goals.

The role of education in financial success cannot be ignored. The more you know about personal finance, the better you'll be able to make intelligent decisions. This chapter will discuss the importance of financial education and provide resources for further learning. Whether it's books, online courses, or workshops, investing in your financial education is one of the best investments you can make.

Another important aspect is the role of mindfulness in managing finances. Being mindful of your spending and financial habits can help you make more intentional choices. This chapter will introduce mindfulness techniques that can be applied to your financial life. You can avoid impulsive decisions and focus on what truly matters by staying present and aware.

Reevaluating your financial habits is an ongoing process. It's not something you do once and forget about; it is something you continually work on. This chapter emphasizes the importance of regular check-ins and adjustments. By staying proactive and flexible, you can adapt to changes in your financial situation and continue to make progress toward your goals.

Finally, this chapter will highlight the importance of celebrating your financial wins. Whether it is paying off a debt, reaching a savings goal, or simply sticking to your budget for a month, it is essential to acknowledge and celebrate your achievements. Celebrating your successes can keep you motivated and remind you that you can achieve your financial goals.

Chapter 3: CHASING THE BAG: Financial Self-Assessment Tools

Financial self-assessment tools are like mirrors for your money; they show you exactly where you stand and where you need to go. Utilizing financial planning software is one of the most effective ways to assess your financial health. These tools can help you track your income, expenses, and investments. This chapter will review some of the best financial planning software available and guide you through setting them up. Using these tools lets you get a clear picture of your financial situation and make informed decisions.

Creating personal financial statements is another crucial step in assessing your financial health. These statements show your assets, liabilities, income, and expenses. This chapter will guide you through creating a balance sheet and an income statement. By understanding these documents, you can see exactly where your money is going and identify areas for improvement.

Benchmarking your financial health against goals is essential for tracking progress. This chapter will introduce you to key financial ratios and benchmarks that can help you assess your financial health. Whether it is the debt-to-income ratio, savings rate, or investment growth, these benchmarks provide valuable insights into your financial situation. By comparing your numbers to industry standards, you can see where you stand and what you need to work on.

The role of budgeting in financial assessment cannot be overstated. A budget is like a financial roadmap; it shows you where your money is going and helps you stay on track. This chapter will guide you through the process of creating a detailed budget. By tracking your income and expenses, you can identify areas where you can cut back and save more. A well-maintained budget is a powerful tool for financial success.

Understanding your net worth is another crucial aspect of financial assessment. Your net worth is the difference between your assets and liabilities. This chapter will guide you through calculating your net worth and tracking it over time. By understanding your net worth, you can see the overall picture of your financial health and make informed decisions.

The importance of tracking expenses cannot be overstated. Knowing where your money is going is the first step toward controlling it. This chapter will introduce you to different methods of tracking expenses, from manual tracking to using apps and software. By staying on top of your spending, you can identify problem areas and make necessary adjustments.

Another critical aspect is understanding your cash flow. Cash flow is the money coming in and going out of your accounts. This chapter will guide you through creating and analyzing a cash flow statement. By understanding,  you can ensure you have enough money to cover your expenses and avoid financial stress.

Credit reports and scores are essential tools for assessing your financial health. Your credit score affects your ability to get loans, credit cards, and even rent an apartment. This chapter will guide you through the process of obtaining and understanding your credit report and score. By staying on top of your credit, you can improve it and ensure that you are in an advantageous position to access credit when you need it.

Another useful tool is the debt-to-income ratio. This ratio compares your monthly debt payments to your monthly income. This chapter will guide you through the process of calculating your debt-to-income ratio and understanding its implications. By keeping your debt-to-income ratio in check, you can ensure that you are not overburdened by debt and can comfortably manage your finances.

On-trial insurance is another essential aspect of the financial assessment. Whether it is health insurance, life insurance, or property insurance, having the right coverage is critical for forecasting your financial health. This chapter will guide you through evaluating your insurance needs and finding the right policies. By having the right insurance, you can protect yourself from unexpected expenses and ensure financial stability.

Another critical tool is investment analysis. Understanding your investments and their performance is essential for long-term financial success. This chapter will guide you through the process of evaluating your investment portfolio and making necessary adjustments. By understanding your investments, you can ensure that they align with your financial goals and risk tolerance.

The role of financial advisors in self-assessment cannot be ignored. Sometimes, it is helpful to get an outside perspective on your finances. This chapter will discuss the benefits of working with a financial advisor and how to find the right one. By getting professional advice, you can ensure you are on the right track and make informed decisions.

Another important aspect is the role of financial goals in self-assessment. Setting and tracking financial goals is essential for staying motivated and making progress. This chapter will guide you through setting realistic, achievable goals. Achievable, clear goals focused and motivated what you know about them.

Finally, this chapter will emphasize the importance of regular financial check-ups. Just like you need regular health check-ups, your finances need regular assessments. This chapter will provide a schedule for regular financial check-ups and the key areas to review. By staying proactive and regularly assessing your finances, you can ensure you are on track for finances.

Chapter 4: SECURING THE BAG: Emergency Funds and Savings Strategies

Having an emergency fund is like having a superhero in your wallet; it swoops in to save the day when life throws unexpected expenses your way. The importance of having a safety net cannot be overstated. Whether it is a medical emergency, car repair, or job loss, having an emergency fund can mean the difference between a minor setback and a major fiscal crisis. This chapter will guide you through setting up and maintaining an emergency fund. Think of it as your financial shield against life's unpredictability.

The first step in building an emergency fund is determining how much you need to save. This chapter will help you calculate your target amount based on your monthly expenses. Experts recommend keeping three to seven months' worth of costs, which can vary depending on your situation. By understanding your needs, you can set a realistic savings goal that provides a sufficient safety net.

Once you have set your target amount, the next step is to start saving. This chapter will provide practical tips for finding extra money for your emergency fund. From cutting back on non-essential expenses to finding ways to increase your income, there are countless ways to free up cash for savings. The key is to prioritize saving and start small if necessary. Every little bit adds up over time.

Automating your savings is one of the most effective strategies for building an emergency fund. This chapter will guide you through setting up automatic transfers to your savings account. By automating your savings, you ensure that money is set aside regularly without thinking about it. This "set it and forget it" approach can help you build your fund quickly and consistently.

Another vital aspect is choosing the correct account for your emergency fund. This chapter will discuss the different available savings accounts pros and cons of different savings accounts. High-yield savings accounts, money market accounts, and certificates of deposit are all options to consider. The goal is to find an account that offers an abundance of accessibility and interest.

Maintaining your emergency fund is just as important as building it. This chapter will provide tips for keeping your fund intact and avoiding the temptation to dip into it for non-emergencies. By setting clear rules for what constitutes an emergency, you can ensure that your fund is always available when you truly need it.

Savings strategies extend beyond emergency funds. This chapter will explore different techniques for building and maintaining savings for various goals. Whether saving for a vacation, a new car, or a down payment on a house, having a clear strategy can help you achieve your financial goals. There is countless ways500th e practical, from the effective to the envelope system, where the active savings strategy is to pay yourself first. This means setting aside a portion of your income for savings before paying bills or other expenses. This chapter will guide you through prioritizing savings and making it a non-negotiable part of your budget. By paying yourself first, you ensure that savings are always a priority.

Another important aspect is setting specific savings goals. Having clear, measurable goals can keep you motivated and focused. This chapter will guide you through the process of Specific, Measurable, Achievable, Relevant, Time-bound) goals for your savings. By having specific targets, you can track your progress and stay motivated.

The role of budgeting in savings cannot be overstated. A budget helps you allocate your income to different expenses, including Savings. This chapter will guide you through creating a budget that includes savings as a critical component. By tracking your income and expenses, you can find areas where you can cut back and save more.

Understanding the importance of compound interest is crucial for effective savings. This chapter will explain how compound interest works and how it can help your savings grow over time. By starting early and saving regularly, you can take advantage of the power of compound interest to build a substantial savings over time.

Another effective strategy is to save windfalls and unexpected income. Whether it is a tax refund, bonus, or gift, putting unexpected money into savings can help you reach your goals faster. This chapter will provide tips for making the most of windfalls and ensuring that they contribute to your financial security.

The role of lifestyle changes in saving money cannot be ignored. This chapter will explore separate ways to reduce your living expenses and save more. From cooking at home to finding free entertainment, there are countless ways to enjoy life without breaking the bank. By making small lifestyle changes, you can free up more money for savings.

The importance of tracking your savings progress cannot be overstated. This chapter will provide tips for monitoring your savings and staying motivated. Whether you use a spreadsheet or app or simply check your account balance regularly, tracking your progress can keep you focused and motivated. Seeing your savings grow will encourage you to keep going.

Finally, this chapter will emphasize the importance of celebrating your savings milestones. Whether you reach a specific savings goal or simply stick to your budget for a month, it is important to acknowledge and celebrate your achievements. Celebrating your successes can keep you motivated and remind you that you can achieve your financial goals.

Chapter 5: CHASING THE BAG: Exploring Alternative Revenue Streams

Exploring alternative revenue streams is like planting multiple trees; it diversifies your income sources and provides financial stability. One of the  most popular ways to create additional income is through passive income ideas. Passive income is money earned with little to no effort. This chapter will explore various passive income opportunities, from dividend-paying stocks to rental properties. By diversifying your income, you can reduce your financial risk and create a more stable economic future.

Starting a small business or side hustle is another effective way to generate additional income. This chapter will guide you through identifying profitable side hustle ideas and turning them into reality. Whether it is selling handmade crafts on Etsy, offering freelance services, or starting a blog, there are countless ways to monetize your skills and passions. By dedicating a week to your side hustle, you can create a significant additional income stream.

Leveraging your skills for freelance opportunities is another fantastic way to increase your income. This chapter will explore different freelance platforms and how to get started. Whether you are a writer, designer, or programmer, there are countless opportunities to find freelance work. You can earn extra income on your own terms by leveraging your skills.

Another effective strategy is investing in real estate. This chapter will guide you through finding and evaluating rental properties. Real estate can provide a steady stream of passive income and long-term wealth. By understanding the basics of real estate investing, you can make informed decisions and build a profitable portfolio.

The role of technology in generating alternative revenue streams cannot be overstated. This chapter will explore different online platforms and tools that can help you create additional income. From selling digital products to creating online courses, technology has made monetizing your skills and knowledge more accessible than ever. You can create scalable income streams that grow over time by leveraging technology.

Investing in dividend-paying stocks is another effective way to create passive income. This chapter will guide you through selecting and investing in dividend stocks. By building a portfolio of dividend-paying stocks, you can create a steady make of passive income that grows over time. Understanding the basics of stock investing and the importance of diversification can help you build a profitable portfolio.

Another important aspect is understanding the gig economy. This chapter will explore different gig  economy opportunities, from ridesharing to food delivery. The gig economy offers flexible work opportunities that can provide additional income. By understanding the pros and cons of gig work, you can find opportunities that fit your lifestyle and financial goals.

Creating and selling digital products is another fantastic way to generate additional income. This chapter will guide you through the process of creating and marketing digital products, such as eBooks, courses, and printables. Digital products have low overhead costs and can be sold to a global audience. By leveraging your expertise, you can create valuable products that generate passive income.

Another effective strategy is to invest in peer-to-peer lending by leveraging your expertise. This chapter will explore different peer-to-peer lending platforms and how to get started. Peer-to-peer lending allows you to earn interest by lending money to individuals or small businesses. Understanding the risks and rewards will enable you to create a diversified lending portfolio that generates passive income.

Affiliate marketing is another fashionable way to create additional income. This chapter will guide you through finding and promoting affiliate products. By partnering with companies and promoting their products, you can earn commissions on sales. Understanding the basics of affiliate marketing and how to choose the right products can help you create a profitable income stream.

Another important aspect is creating a diversified investment portfolio. This chapter will guide you through the process of creating a unified portfolio that includes stocks, bonds, real estate, and other assets. By diversifying your investments, you can reduce risk and create multiple income streams. Understanding the importance of asset allocation and rebalancing can help you build a profitable portfolio.

The role of education in creating alternative revenue streams cannot be ignored. This chapter will provide resources for further learning and development. Whether taking courses, reading books, or attending workshops, investing in your education can open new income opportunities. By creating income opportunities and developing your skills, you can stay ahead of the curve and create new income streams.

Another effective strategy is monetizing a hobby. This chapter will explore separate ways to turn your hobbies into income. Whether photography, gardening, or playing music, there are countless ways to monetize your passions. By finding creative ways to make money from your hobbies, you can enjoy doing what you love while generating additional income.

The importance of networking cannot be overstated. This chapter will explore building and leveraging your network to create income opportunities. Whether attending try events, joining professional associations, or simply connecting with others online, networking can open new opportunities; you can create a set system that helps you achieve your financial goals.

Finally, this chapter emphasizes the importance of action. Exploring alternative revenue streams is all about being proactive and taking initiative. This chapter provides tips and strategies for getting started and staying motivated. By taking small steps each day, you can create new income streams and achieve financial stability.

Chapter 6: Basic Principles of Financial Planning

Financial planning is like a GPS for your money; it helps you navigate from  where you are to where you want to be. Creating a personalized financial plan is the first step toward economic success. This chapter will guide you through setting short-term and long-term financial goals. By having clear, achievable goals, you can stay focused and motivated on your financial journey.

Setting short-term goals is crucial for immediate financial stability. This chapter will provide tips for identifying and prioritizing short-term goals, such as paying off debt, building an emergency fund, or saving for a vacation. By focusing on short-term goals, you can achieve quick wins that boost your confidence and set the stage for long-term success.

Long-term goals are equally important for achieving financial independence. This chapter will guide you through short-term goals, such as saving for retirement, buying a home, or starting a business. By having an unobstructed vision of your future, you can make informed decisions that align with your long-term objectives.

Implementing a financial timeline is essential for staying on track. This chapter will introduce you to different financial timelines and how to create one that works for you. By breaking down your goals, you can stay organized and focused by manageable steps and setting deadlines; you can stay organized and find a roadmap for your financial journey, helping you stay on track and make steady progress.

Understanding the importance of budgeting is crucial for effective financial planning. A budget helps you allocate your income towards different expenses and savings goals. This chapter will guide you through the process of creating a detailed budget. You can find areas where you can cut back and save more by tracking your income and expenses. A well-maintained budget is a powerful tool for financial success.

The role of saving in financial planning cannot be overstated. This chapter will explore different saving strategies and techniques. Whether it is setting up automatic transfers to a  savings account, using the envelope system, or implementing the 50/30/20 rule, there are countless ways to save effectively. By making saving a priority, you can build a strong financial foundation.

Investing is another crucial aspect of financial planning. This chapter will introduce you to different investment vehicles and strategies. Whether it is stocks, bonds, real estate, or mutual funds, investing can help you grow your wealth over time. By understanding the basics of investing and the importance of diversification, you can make informed decisions that align with your financial goals.

Understanding risk management is crucial for effective financial planning. This chapter will explore ways to manage financial risks, such as insurance, emergency funds, and diversification. By having a risk management plan in place, you can protect yourself from unexpected expenses and ensure financial stability.

The importance of regular financial reviews cannot be overstated. This chapter will guide you through the process of conducting regular financial check-ups. By reviewing your financial plan regularly, you can make necessary adjustments and stay on track toward your goals. Regular reviews help you stay proactive and adapt to changes in your financial situation.

Another critical aspect is understanding taxes and how they impact your financial plan. This chapter will provide an overview of tax strategies and how to minimize tax liability. By understanding the basics of taxes and how to Plan, you can keep more of your hard-earned money and achieve your financial goals faster.

The role of retirement planning in financial planning cannot be ignored. This chapter will guide you through the process of creating a retirement plan. Understanding how much you need to save and where to invest can ensure that you are on track for a comfortable retirement. Planning for retirement is essential for long-term financial stability.

Another critical aspect is understanding the importance of estate planning. This chapter will provide an overview of estate planning tools, such as wills, trusts, and powers of attorney. Having an estate plan in place, you can ensure that your assets are distributed according to your wishes and that your loved ones are included. The importance of financial education in financial planning cannot be overstated. This chapter will provide resources for further learning and development. Whether taking courses, reading books, or attending workshops, investing in your financial education can open new opportunities and help you make informed decisions. By continuously learning and developing your economic knowledge, you can stay ahead of the curve and achieve your financial goals.

Another critical aspect is understanding the role of financial advisors in financial planning. This chapter will discuss the benefits of working with a financial advisor and how to find the right one. By getting professional advice, you can ensure you are on the right track and making informed decisions. A financial advisor can provide personalized advice, guidance, and strategies to help you navigate complex financial situations.

Finally, this chapter will emphasize the importance of acting. Financial planning is all about being proactive and taking initiative. This chapter will provide tips and strategies for getting started and staying motivated. By taking small steps each day, you can create a solid financial plan and achieve your goals.

Chapter 7: Understanding Credit and Loans

Understanding credit and loans is like having a map for your financial journey; it helps you navigate the world of borrowing and ensures you make  informed decisions. Credit is a powerful economic tool but can also be a double-edged sword. This chapter will guide you through the basics of credit, how it works, and how to use it responsibly. By understanding credit, you can build a strong credit history and access the financial resources you need.

Understanding how credit works is the first step in understanding its importance. This chapter will explain the concept of credit, how it is measured, and how it impacts your financial life. Understanding these components, from credit scores to credit reports, can help you make informed decisions and avoid common pitfalls.

Several types of loans have different purposes. This chapter will provide overviews of loan types, such as personal loans, mortgages, auto loans, and student loans. By understanding the differences and uses of each type of loan, you can choose the right one for your needs and avoid unnecessary debt.

Managing credit responsibly is crucial for maintaining financial health. This chapter will provide tips and strategies for using credit wisely. From making timely payments to keeping your credit utilization low, several ways to manage your credit effectively exist. By being responsible with your credit, you can build a strong credit history and avoid financial stress.

Understanding interest rates is another important aspect of managing credit and loans. This chapter will explain how interest rates work and how they affect your borrowing costs. By understanding the impact of interest rates, you can make informed decisions and choose the best loan options for your needs.

The role of credit scores in accessing credit cannot be overstated. This chapter will guide you through the process of improving your credit score. 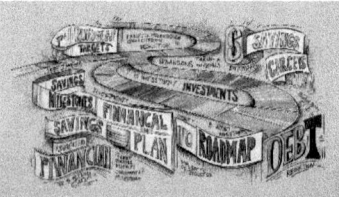 Whether it is paying off debt, correcting errors on your credit report, or establishing a positive credit history, there are several ways to boost your score. A strong credit score opens more overborrowing opportunities and can be beneficial overall.

Another critical aspect is understanding the terms and conditions of loans. This chapter will guide you through reading and understanding loan agreements. From interest rates to repayment terms, understanding the fine print can help you avoid surprises and make informed decisions. By knowing what you are signing up for, you can ensure you get the best deal.

The importance of debt management cannot be overstated. This chapter will provide tips and strategies for managing and reducing debt. There are several ways to manage debt effectively, whether creating a debt repayment plan, consolidating loans, or negotiating with creditors. By staying on top of your debt, you can avoid financial stress and achieve economic stability.

Another critical aspect is understanding the impact of loans on your financial plan. This chapter will explore how borrowing affects your overall financial health and how to incorporate loans into your financial plan. By understanding the role of loans in your monetary strategy, you can make informed decisions and achieve your financial goals.

Building credit is crucial. This chapter provides tips for establishing and maintaining a positive credit history. Whether using a secured credit card, making timely payments, or keeping your credit utilization low, there are several ways to build credit. A strong credit history opens more opportunities and can save money on borrowing costs.

Understanding the role of credit in major purchases is crucial. This chapter will guide you through the process of using credit for major purchases, such as buying a home or car. By understanding the impact of credit on these transactions, you can make informed decisions and ensure that you are getting the best deal.

Another important aspect is understanding the impact of credit on renting and employment. This chapter will explore how credit affects your ability to rent an apartment or get a job. By understanding these implications, you can take steps to improve your credit and ensure that it does not hinder your opportunities.

The role of financial education in understanding credit and loans cannot be overstated. This chapter will provide resources for further learning and development. Whether taking courses, reading books, or attending workshops, investing in your financial education can help you make informed decisions and avoid common pitfalls. By continuously learning about credit and loans, you can stay ahead of the curve and achieve your financial goals.

Another critical aspect is understanding the role of financial advisors in managing credit and loans. This chapter will discuss the benefits of working with a financial advisor and how to find the right one. By getting professional advice, you can ensure you are making informed decisions and managing your credit effectively. A financial advisor can provide personalized guidance and strategies to help you navigate the world of credit and loans.

Finally, this chapter will emphasize the importance of acting. Understanding credit and loans is all about being proactive and taking initiative. This chapter will provide tips and strategies for getting started and staying motivated. You can build a strong credit history and manage your loans effectively by taking small steps each day.

Chapter 8: SECURING THE BAG: Effective Money Management Systems

Effective money management systems are like a car's engine: They keep everything running smoothly and ensure you reach your destination. Budgeting tools and apps are essential for  tracking your income and expenses. This chapter will review some of the best budgeting tools and apps and guide you through setting them up. Using these tools lets you stay on top of your finances and make informed decisions.

Systems for tracking expenses are crucial for effective money management. This chapter will introduce you to different methods of tracking expenses, from manual tracking to using apps and software. By staying on top of your spending, you can identify problem areas and make necessary adjustments. Tracking your expenses is the first step towards controlling your money.

Tips for optimizing cash flow are essential for maintaining financial stability. This chapter will provide practical tips for improving your cash flow. Whether negotiating better payment terms, reducing expenses, or finding ways to increase income, there are several ways to optimize cash flow. By managing your cash flow effectively, you can ensure that you have enough money to cover your expenses.

The role of budgeting in money management cannot be overstated. A budget helps you allocate your income towards different expenses and savings goals. This chapter will guide you through the process of creating a detailed budget. By tracking your 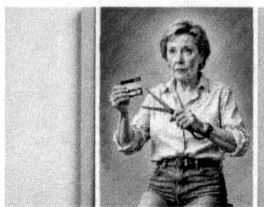 income, you can cut back and save more. A well-maintained budget by monitoring your income and expenses budget is a powerful tool for financial success.

Understanding the importance of saving is crucial for effective money management. This chapter will explore different saving strategies and techniques. Whether it is setting up automatic transfers to a savings account, using the envelope system, or implementing the 50/30/20 rule, there are countless ways to save effectively. By making saving a priority, you can build a strong financial foundation.

Investing is another crucial aspect of money management. This chapter will introduce you to different investment vehicles and strategies. Whether it is stocks, bonds, real estate, or mutual funds, investing can help you grow your wealth over time. By understanding the basics of investing and the importance of diversification, you can make informed decisions that align with your financial goals.

Understanding risk management is crucial for effective money management. This chapter will explore ways to manage financial risks, such as insurance, emergency funds, and diversification. By having a risk management plan in place, you can protect yourself from unexpected expenses and ensure financial stability.

The importance of regular financial reviews cannot be overstated. This chapter will guide you through the process of conducting regular financial check-ups. By reviewing your financial plan regularly, you can make necessary adjustments and stay on track toward your goals. Regular reviews help you stay proactive and adapt to changes in your financial situation.

Another critical aspect is understanding taxes and how they impact your financial plan. This chapter will provide an overview of tax strategies and how to minimize tax liability. By understanding the basics of taxes and how to plan for them, you can keep more of your hard-earned money and achieve your financial goals faster.

The role of retirement planning in money management cannot be ignored. This chapter will guide you through the process of creating a retirement plan. By understanding how much to save and where to invest, you will ensure that you are on track for a comfortable retirement. Planning for retirement is essential for long-term financial stability.

Another critical aspect is understanding the importance of estate planning. This chapter will provide an overview of estate planning tools, such as wills, trusts, and powers of attorney.

Having an estate plan in place can ensure that your assets are distributed according to your wishes and that your loved ones are taken care of.

The importance of financial education in money management cannot be overstated. This chapter will provide resources for further learning and development. Whether taking courses, reading books, or attending workshops, investing in your financial education can open new opportunities and help you make informed decisions. By continuously learning and developing your financial knowledge, you can stay ahead of the curve and achieve your financial goals.

Another critical aspect is understanding the role of financial advisors in money management. This chapter will discuss the benefits of working with a financial advisor and how to find the right one. By getting professional advice, you can ensure you are on the right track and making informed decisions. A financial advisor can provide personalized guidance and strategies to help you navigate complex financial situations.

Finally, this chapter will emphasize the importance of acting. Money management is all about being proactive and taking initiative. This chapter will provide tips and strategies for getting started and staying motivated. By taking small steps each day, you can create a solid financial plan and achieve your goals.

Chapter 9: SECURING THE BAG: Planning for the Unexpected

Planning for the unexpected is like having an umbrella on a sunny day; it might seem unnecessary until needed. Insurance options and their importance cannot be overstated. Whether it is health insurance, life insurance, or property insurance, having the right coverage is essential for protecting your financial health. This chapter will guide you through evaluating your insurance needs and finding the right policies.

Preparing for life changes, such as marriage, children, or retirement, is another crucial aspect of planning for the unexpected. This chapter will provide tips and strategies for planning for major life events. By being proactive and planning, you can ensure that you are financially prepared for whatever life throws your way.

Creating a contingency plan is essential for financial stability. This chapter will guide you through the process of creating a contingency plan for different scenarios, such as job loss, medical emergencies, or natural disasters. By having a plan in place, you can ensure that you are prepared for the unexpected and can navigate financial challenges with confidence.

The role of emergency funds in planning for the unexpected cannot be overstated. This chapter will provide tips for building and maintaining an 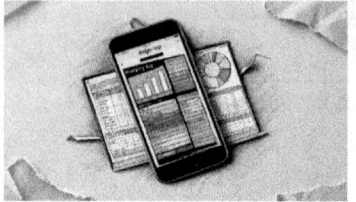 emergency fund. By having a financial cushion, you can protect yourself from unexpected expenses and ensure financial stability. An emergency fund is a crucial part of any contingency plan.

Understanding the importance of diversification in planning for the unexpected is crucial. This chapter will explore separate ways to diversify your income and investments. Multiple income streams and a diversified investment portfolio can reduce financial risk and create a more stable economic future.

The importance of staying informed cannot be ignored. This chapter will provide tips for staying informed about potential risks and changes in your financial situation. Whether it is keeping up with news, reviewing your financial plan regularly, or seeking professional advice, staying informed is crucial for planning for the unexpected.

Another critical aspect is understanding the role of financial education in planning for the unexpected. This chapter will provide resources for further learning and development. Whether taking courses, reading books, or attending workshops, investing in your financial education can help you make informed decisions and avoid common pitfalls. By continuously learning about potential risks and how to manage them, you can stay ahead of the curve and ensure financial stability.

The role of financial advisors in planning for the unexpected cannot be ignored. This chapter will discuss the benefits of working with a financial advisor and how to find the right one. By getting professional advice, you can ensure that you are prepared for the unexpected and have a solid plan. A financial advisor can provide personalized advice and guidance to help you navigate complex financial situations.

Another critical aspect is understanding the impact of taxes on planning for the unexpected. This chapter will provide an overview of tax strategies and how to minimize tax liability. By understanding the basics of taxes and how to plan for them, you can keep more of your hard-earned money and ensure financial stability.

Understanding the importance of regular financial reviews in planning for the unexpected cannot be overstated. This chapter will guide you through the process of conducting regular financial check-ups. Reviewing your financial plan regularly allows you to adjust and stay on track toward your goals. Regular reviews help you stay proactive and adapt to changes in your financial situation.

Budgeting is crucial in planning for the unexpected. This chapter will guide you through creating a detailed budget with a contingency plan. By tracking your income and expenses and allocating funds for unforeseen events, you can ensure you are prepared for the unexpected.

Understanding the importance of saving in planning for the unexpected is crucial. This chapter will explore different saving strategies and techniques. Whether it is setting up auto transfers to a savings account, using the envelope system, or implementing the 50/30/20 rule, there are countless ways to save effectively. By making saving a priority, you can build a solid financial foundation. The importance of investing in planning for the unexpected cannot be overstated. This chapter will introduce you to different investment vehicles and strategies. Whether it is stocks, bonds, real estate, or mutual funds, investing can help you grow your wealth over time. By understanding the basics of investing and the importance of diversification, you can make informed decisions that align with your financial goals.

Finally, this chapter will emphasize the importance of acting. Planning for the unexpected is all about being proactive and taking initiative. This chapter will provide tips and strategies for getting started and staying motivated. By taking small steps daily, you can create a solid financial plan and ensure you are prepared for whatever life throws your way.

Chapter 10: SECURING THE BAG: Achieving Financial Independence

Achieving financial independence is like reaching the summit of a mountain; it is the culmination of hard work, planning, and perseverance.  Strategies for wealth accumulation are essential for achieving financial independence. This chapter will explore different wealth-building techniques, from saving and investing to creating multiple income streams. By understanding these strategies, you can plan for achieving financial independence.

Creating multiple income streams is crucial for financial independence. This chapter will guide you through identifying and developing additional income sources. Whether it is starting a hustle, investing in real estate, or creating passive income, there are countless ways to diversify your income. Multiple income streams can reduce your finances and create a more stable economic future.

Steps towards achieving and maintaining financial freedom are essential for long-term success. This chapter provides a step-by-step guide for achieving financial independence. From setting goals and creating a financial plan to staying disciplined and making necessary adjustments, it provides practical tips and strategies for achieving and maintaining financial freedom.

Understanding the importance of saving in achieving financial independence cannot be overstated. This chapter will explore different  saving strategies and techniques. Whether it is setting up automatic transfers to a savings account, using the envelope system, or implementing the 50/30/20 rule, there are countless ways to save effectively. By making saving a priority, you can build a strong financial foundation.

Investing is another crucial aspect of achieving financial independence. This chapter will introduce you to different investment vehicles and strategies. Whether it is stocks, bonds, real estate, or mutual funds, investing can help you grow your wealth over time. By understanding the basics of investing and the importance of diversification, you can make informed decisions that align with your financial goals.

Understanding risk management is crucial for achieving financial independence. This chapter will explore ways to manage financial risks, such as insurance, emergency funds, and diversification. By having a risk management plan in place, you can protect yourself from unexpected expenses and ensure financial stability.

The importance of regular financial reviews cannot be overstated. This chapter will guide you through the process of conducting regular financial check-ups. Reviewing your financial plan regularly allows you to make necessary adjustments and stay on  track toward your goals. Regular reviews help you stay proactive and adapt to changes in your financial situation.

Another critical aspect is understanding taxes and how they impact your financial plan. This chapter will provide an overview of tax strategies and how to minimize tax liability. By understanding the basics of taxes and how to plan for them, you can keep more of your hard-earned money and achieve your financial goals faster.

The role of retirement planning in achieving financial independence cannot be ignored. This chapter will guide you through the process of creating a retirement plan. By understanding how much you need to save and where to invest, you can ensure that you are on track for a comfortable retirement. Planning for retirement is essential for long-term financial stability.

Another key aspect is understanding the importance of estate planning. This chapter will provide an overview of different estate planning tools, such as wills, trusts, and powers of attorney. By having an estate plan in place, you can ensure that your assets are distributed according to your wishes and that your loved ones are taken care of.

The importance of financial education in achieving financial independence cannot be overstated.  This chapter will provide resources for further learning and development. Whether it is taking courses, reading books, or attending workshops, investing in your financial education can open new opportunities and help you make informed decisions. By continuously learning and developing your financial knowledge, you can stay ahead of the curve and achieve your financial goals.

Another critical aspect is understanding the role of financial advisors in achieving economic independence. This chapter will discuss the benefits of working with a financial advisor and how to find the right one. By getting professional advice, you can ensure you are on the right track and making informed decisions. A financial advisor can provide personalized guidance and strategies to help you navigate complex financial situations.

Finally, this chapter emphasizes the importance of action. Achieving financial independence is all about being proactive and taking initiative. This chapter provides tips and strategies for getting started and staying motivated. By taking small steps each day, you can create a solid financial plan and achieve your goals.

Conclusion

In conclusion, "Fumbling the Bag, Chasing the Bag, Securing the Bag: From Setbacks to Comebacks: Your Path to Financial Freedom" ties together a comprehensive roadmap for transforming financial missteps into success stories.  Throughout this book, we have explored the anatomy of economic failures, reevaluated financial habits, and examined various self-assessment tools, all crucial for understanding where you stand financially and where you need to go.

The journey begins with recognizing the root causes of financial setbacks. Understanding these causes is essential because it allows you to address the underlying issues that lead to financial distress. By identifying psychological triggers and poor financial habits, you can begin to make changes that will set you on the path to financial recovery. This awareness is the first step in turning a financial fumble into an opportunity for growth.

Reevaluating your financial habits is the next crucial step. Rude habits like impulse buying and living beyond your means can quickly drain your resources. You can develop healthier financial behaviors by analyzing your spending patterns and making conscious changes. This re-evaluation process is like hitting the reset button on your financial life, allowing you to start fresh with a clear plan and purpose.

Financial self-assessment tools are indispensable for gaining a clear picture of your financial health. Tools like financial planning software, personal financial statements, and  benchmarking against goals provide you with the data needed to make informed decisions. These tools act as a financial mirror, reflecting your current situation and highlighting areas that need improvement. They are essential for tracking progress and staying accountable to your goals.

Emergency funds and savings strategies are vital components of financial security. A safety net ensures you are prepared for unexpected expenses, preventing minor setbacks from becoming major economic crises. Building an emergency fund and adopting effective savings strategies create a buffer that allows you to navigate life's uncertainties confidently.

Alternative revenue streams diversify your income and reduce financial risk. Side hustles, passive income, and freelance opportunities can provide additional financial stability. By leveraging your skills and interests, you can create multiple income streams that enhance your financial security and offer more flexibility in managing your finances.

The basic principles of financial planning, such as setting goals, budgeting, saving, and investing, form the foundation of economic success. These principles guide your financial decisions and help you focus on your long-term financial plan. By implementing solid financial plans, you can steadily progress toward achieving your financial goals.

Understanding credit and loans is essential for making informed borrowing decisions. Credit can be a powerful tool when used responsibly, but it can also lead to financial trouble if mismanaged. By understanding how credit works, managing it wisely, and using it to your advantage, you can build a strong credit history and access the financial resources you need.

Effective money management systems ensure that your financial engine runs smoothly. Budgeting tools, expense tracking methods, and cash flow optimization techniques help you stay on top of your finances. These systems provide the structure needed to manage your money effectively, allowing you to make informed decisions and avoid financial pitfalls.

Planning for the unexpected is crucial for maintaining financial  stability. Life is full of surprises, and a contingency plan ensures you are prepared for whatever comes your way. Insurance, emergency funds, and diversification strategies provide a safety net that protects your financial health and allows you to recover quickly from setbacks.

The goal of financial planning is financial independence, which is linked to wealth. You can achieve financial freedom through multiple income streams and managing risks; you can achieve financial freedom on your terms, pursue your passions, and enjoy the peace of mind of financial security.

Throughout this book, the recurring theme has been the transformation of setbacks into comebacks. Whether it is overcoming debt, building savings, or investing for the future, each chapter has provided practical strategies for turning financial challenges into opportunities for growth. This transformation is at the heart of "Fumbling the Bag, Chasing the Bag, Securing the Bag."

The process of fumbling the bag represents the financial missteps and mistakes that everyone experiences at some point. These mistakes can be frustrating and disheartening, but they also provide valuable lessons. By acknowledging and learning from these mistakes, you can gain the knowledge and resilience needed to improve your financial situation.

Chasing the bag is about taking proactive steps to improve your financial health. This involves setting goals, creating a plan, and acting. It is about being assertive and focused on your financial endeavors, whether starting a side hustle, investing in your education, or finding new ways to save. Chasing the bag is a continuous effort to better your financial position.

Securing the bag is the culmination of your efforts. It is about achieving financial stability and independence through disciplined planning and execution. Securing the bag means having a solid financial foundation,  multiple income streams, and a safety net to protect against unforeseen events. It is the point where you can confidently say you have control over your financial future.

The concept of turning setbacks into comebacks applies to economic management. From managing debt and building savings to investing and planning for retirement, each step of the journey involves overcoming challenges and making progress towards your goals. This resilience and determination are what give you ultimate financial freedom.

The principles outlined in this book are essential in day-to-day business. Economic management is a critical aspect of running a successful business, and the strategies discussed can help  you make informed decisions, manage cash flow, and plan. Whether you are a small business owner or an entrepreneur, applying these principles can lead to sustainable success.

The importance of financial education cannot be overstated. You can 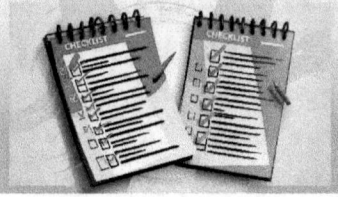 make informed decisions and avoid common pitfalls by continuously learning and developing your financial knowledge. This book has provided a wealth of information and resources to help you on your journey, but the learning does not stop here. Keep seeking out opportunities to expand your knowledge and improve your financial skills.

Finally, the journey to financial freedom is ongoing. It is not about achieving a specific milestone and then stopping; it is about continuously striving for improvement and growth. Applying the principles and strategies discussed in this book, you can build a solid financial foundation and achieve your goals. Remember, setbacks are just opportunities for comebacks, and with the right mindset and tools, you can secure the bag and enjoy financial freedom.

FUMBLING THE BAG, CHASING THE BAG, SECURIING THE BAG 💰

YOUR PATH TO FINANCIAL FREEDOM

In summary, "Fumbling the Bag, Chasing the Bag, Securing the Bag: From Setbacks to Comebacks: Your Path to Financial Freedom" provides a comprehensive guide to turning financial missteps into success stories. You can achieve economic stability and independence by understanding the root causes of financial setbacks, reevaluating your habits, using self-assessment tools, and implementing practical strategies. This book is your companion on the journey to financial freedom, providing the knowledge, motivation, and support you need to succeed.

Check Out A Book Bundle From
Brian's Other Famous Titles
"How To Get Past The Gatekeepers and
Get To Your Goal In Life:
A Personal Guide to Being Persistent"

Bibliography

1. **Covey, Stephen R.** *The 7 Habits of Highly Effective People: Powerful Lessons in Personal Change*. Simon & Schuster, 1989.

2. **Hill, Napoleon.** *Think and Grow Rich*. The Ralston Society, 1937.

3. **Kiyosaki, Robert T.** *Rich Dad Poor Dad: What the Rich Teach Their Kids About Money That the Poor and Middle Class Do Not!*. Plata Publishing, 1997.

4. **Tracy, Brian.** *Goals!: How to Get Everything You Want Faster Than You Ever Thought Possible*. Berrett-Koehler Publishers, 2003.

5. **Sinek, Simon.** *Start with Why: How Great Leaders Inspire Everyone to Take Action*. Portfolio, 2009.

6. **Dweck, Carol S.** *Mindset: The New Psychology of Success*. Ballantine Books, 2006.

7. **Vaynerchuk, Gary.** *Crush It!: Why NOW Is the Time to Cash In on Your Passion*. HarperStudio, 2009.

8. **Cardone, Grant.** *The 10X Rule: The Only Difference Between Success and Failure*. Wiley, 2011.

9. **Ferriss, Timothy.** *The 4-Hour Workweek: Escape 9-5, Live Anywhere, and Join the New Rich*. Crown Publishing Group, 2007.

10. **Thiel, Peter.** *Zero to One: Notes on Startups, or How to Build the Future*. Crown Business, 2014.

11. **Collins, Jim.** *Good to Great: Why Some Companies Make the Leap... and Others Don't*. HarperBusiness, 2001.

12. **Schultz, Howard, and Joanne Gordon.** *Onward: How Starbucks Fought for Its Life without Losing Its Soul*. Rodale Books, 2011.

13. **Maxwell, John C.** *The 21 Irrefutable Laws of Leadership: Follow Them and People Will Follow You*. Thomas Nelson, 1998.

14. **Sincero, Jen.** *You Are a Badass at Making Money: Master the Mindset of Wealth*. Viking, 2017.

15. **Dalio, Ray.** *Principles: Life and Work*. Simon & Schuster, 2017.

NOTES...

www.ingramcontent.com/pod-product-compliance
Lightning Source LLC
Chambersburg PA
CBHW071936210526
45479CB00002B/710